The THOMAS KINKADE Cookbook

A JOURNEY OF CULINARY MEMORIES

THOMAS AND NANETTE KINKADE

Contents

102 *Looking for Memories*

City by the Bay

Introduction

Our family has experienced some fabulous adventures that leave us with lovely memories. Thom remembers with his eye, his brush and his canvas—many of his fondest memories are preserved as paintings for your pleasure in this book.

In addition, our family adventures are highlighted by lovely meals shared together. The senses of savory aroma and taste are linked most powerfully to memory. The rich flavors of seafood pasta reminds me vividly of an evening in Venice and the tangy savor of flame broiled barbecue ribs recalls a glorious Fourth of July barbecue finished with crisp, cold watermelon and then a dazzling fireworks display.

As I tour the world with Thom, I map our travels with a collection of ethnic recipes. In this book, you can travel along with us to exotic ports of call, such as Nice, Paris, London, Venice, the Swiss Alps, Edinburgh, Luxemburg and Portofino. Each is represented by a savory dish or two that make me reminisce about the special flavors of each destination.

The recipes in this book also touch our memories in a variety of other ways. Here are family favorites—some courtesy of my mother, grandmother and aunt; others that have become favorites of my daughters. There are dishes that go along with favorite family activities; others that are featured in local restaurants and favorite places like Carmel and San Francisco.

It is my pleasure to share with you these culinary delights that form such an important part of the Kinkade family heritage. My hope is that these recipes will spark your memories and satisfy your appetite.

Happy eating!

Nanette Kinkade

Nanette Kinkade

Holiday Memories

Pecan Sweet Rolls

1 loaf packaged bread dough
4 tablespoons butter, melted
½ cup sugar
2 teaspoons cinnamon
¼ cup raisins
½ cup chopped pecans
Frosting (see below)

*Y*ou just can't beat the plump Texas pecans that Thom's brother Pat and his wife Laura send us each year. Whether we're all together or apart, each of us feasts on Laura's scrumptious Pecan Sweet Rolls for Christmas morning breakfast.

SERVES 8–12

1. On a lightly floured board, roll dough out to a 8 x 12-inch rectangle. Spread dough with 2 tablespoons melted butter. Mix cinnamon, sugar, raisins and nuts. Sprinkle mixture over dough.

2. Beginning with the 12-inch side, roll tightly in jelly-roll fashion. Cut rolled dough into 12 equal slices. Place slices in lightly buttered muffin pans or 9-inch pie pan. Brush tops with melted butter. Let rise until doubled in size. Bake at 375° for 20–25 minutes or until light brown.

3. Turn out of pan immediately and let cool. Brush tops with any remaining butter.

Frosting

2 cups powdered sugar
2 tablespoons milk
½ teaspoon vanilla

1. Mix ingredients together and spread on rolls.

CHRISTMAS

Victorian Christmas

Standing Rib Roast with Yorkshire Pudding

Some of our favorite traditions began on our travels. On our first trip to England, I discovered Yorkshire pudding and our Christmases have never been the same! Each year, this hearty dish re-awakens memories of that wonderful adventure.

SERVES 12

1. Preheat oven to 325°F.

2. Place roast, fat side up, in a shallow roasting pan and season with salt and pepper. Insert a meat thermometer, taking care to avoid touching bone. Roast, uncovered, until meat thermometer registers 140°F for rare, 160°F for medium and 170°F for well done, approximately 3¼ hours for rare, 4 hours for medium and 4¾ hours for well done.

3. Remove meat from the oven and increase oven temperature to 400°F.

4. Remove meat from pan, cover loosely with foil and reserve pan drippings; pour off ¼ cup of the pan drippings for the pudding.

5. Divide the reserved pan drippings into two 9 x 9-inch baking pans. In a bowl beat together eggs, flour, milk and 1 teaspoon salt until well mixed. Pour batter evenly into both pans and bake for 30 minutes. To serve, carve roast and serve with pudding and pan drippings.

1 beef standing rib roast (8 pounds)
1 teaspoon salt, plus more for seasoning
4 eggs
2 cups all-purpose flour
2 cups milk
1 teaspoon salt
Black pepper

Peppermint Ice Cream Cake

¾   cup unsweetened cocoa
¾   cup boiling water
6   tablespoons butter, melted
1   cup dark brown sugar
½   cup sugar
¾   cup egg substitute
1½ cups all-purpose flour
    (about 6¾ ounces)
½   teaspoon baking powder
½   teaspoon baking soda
½   teaspoon salt
2   teaspoons vanilla
3   cups low-fat peppermint ice
    cream (I recommend Edy's
    or Dreyer's Slow-Churned
    Light), softened
3   cups frozen fat-free whipped
    topping, thawed
⅛   teaspoon peppermint extract
8   peppermint candies, crushed
Cooking spray

One of the great pleasures of raising a family is handing some of my duties on to the children. My girls now do the final assembly for this Christmas Eve family favorite!

SERVES 16

1. Preheat oven to 350°F. Coat two 8-inch round cake pans with cooking spray. Line the bottom of each pan with wax paper.

2. In a bowl, combine cocoa, water and butter. Stir until blended and allow to cool. In a separate bowl, combine sugars and add egg substitute; beat 2 minutes or until light and creamy. Add cocoa mixture and beat for 1 minute. Combine flour, baking powder, baking soda and salt and gradually add to the cocoa mixture. Stir in vanilla.

3. Pour batter into prepared pans and bake for 25 minutes or until a wooden toothpick inserted in the center comes out clean. Cool in pans for 10 minutes on a wire rack. Remove from pans. Wrap in plastic wrap and freeze for 2 hours, or until slightly frozen.

4. Spread ice cream into an 8-inch round cake pan lined with plastic wrap. Cover and freeze for 4 hours or until firm.

5. To assemble cake, place one cake layer, bottom side up, on a cake pedestal or serving platter. Remove ice cream layer from freezer and remove plastic wrap. Place ice cream layer, bottom side up, on top of cake layer. Top with remaining cake layer.

6. Combine whipped topping and peppermint extract and stir until blended. Spread frosting over the top and sides of cake. Sprinkle with crushed peppermint candies and freeze until ready to serve. Allow cake to stand at room temperature for 10 minutes before slicing.

A Holiday Gathering

Morning Dogwood

Crepes

Crepes are among our favorite special occasion foods. They just seem to make any meal festive, and they're perfect for the holidays.

MAKES 12

1. In a bowl, combine flour, baking powder and salt. In a separate bowl, combine milk, eggs and butter; add dry ingredients and beat until smooth.

2. Heat a small skillet over medium heat and add ½ teaspoon butter. Pour scant ¼ cup of the batter into skillet and immediately rotate skillet until a thin film covers bottom of pan.

3. Cook until batter dries, about 45 seconds, flip and cook until edges start to brown slightly. Repeat process, adding butter to the skillet and adjusting heat as necessary. Stack crepes on a plate, placing wax or parchment paper between each layer and cover to keep warm.

4. To serve, place 1 to 2 tablespoons of desired filling in the center of each crepe and roll, taking care to position edge side down. Sprinkle with powdered sugar.

1½ cups all-purpose flour
½ teaspoon baking powder
½ teaspoon salt
2 cups milk
2 eggs
2 tablespoons butter, melted and cooled, plus more for pan
Optional filling ingredients: applesauce, sweetened strawberries, currant jelly and raspberry jam
Powdered sugar

EASTER

Big Apple Dumplings

SAUCE:

2   cups water

1¼ cups sugar

½   teaspoon cinnamon

¼   cup plus 1 tablespoon butter

PASTRY:

2   cups all-purpose flour

½   teaspoon salt

⅔   cup shortening

⅓   cup half-and-half, light cream
    or whole milk

FILLING:

2   tablespoons chopped raisins
    or golden raisins

2   tablespoons chopped walnuts

1   tablespoon honey

2   tablespoons sugar

½   teaspoon cinnamon

6   small cooking apples
    (about 1½ pounds)

SERVES 6

1. Make the sauce: in a medium saucepan combine the water, sugar and cinnamon. Bring to a boil then reduce heat. Simmer, uncovered, for 5 minutes. Add ¼ cup butter, stir to combine and set aside.

2. Make the pastry: in the bowl of a food processor, combine the flour and salt. Mix in shortening until pieces are the size of small peas. Add the half-and-half, light cream, or milk and pulse for 5 seconds, until the dough is moistened. If mixture is still dry, add more liquid, 1 teaspoon at a time, until dough comes together. Remove dough and form into a ball. On a lightly floured surface, roll into an 18 x 12-inch rectangle and divide into 6 squares. For garnishing option, see Note below.

3. Preheat oven to 375°F.

4. Make the filling: in a small mixing bowl, combine the raisins, walnuts and honey. In another small bowl, stir together sugar and cinnamon. Set bowls aside. Peel and core the apples. Place one apple on top of each pastry square. Fill apples centers with raisin mixture, sprinkle with cinnamon sugar and top each with a piece of remaining tablespoon butter. Moisten edges of a pastry square with water, fold corners over apple and pinch to seal. Repeat with remaining apples.

5. Place dumplings in a large baking dish and pour sauce over apples. Bake for 35 minutes or until apples are tender and pastry is golden brown. To serve, plate each apple with some of the sauce from the pan.

NOTE: *If desired, roll pastry slightly larger, cut squares and use excess to make pastry leaves for garnish. Roll out extra pastry and cut into leaf shapes. Place on baking sheet and bake at 375°F until golden brown, about 10 minutes.*

Roast Rack of Lamb

SERVES 4

1. Preheat oven to 375°F.

2. Combine garlic powder, salt and pepper and rub into meat. Place the meat rib-side down in a roasting pan. Roast until meat temperature reaches 140°F for rare, 160°F for medium and 170°F for well done, approximately 45 minutes to 1 hour.

3. Meanwhile, in small saucepan over medium heat, combine apricot preserves and lemon juice and cook until preserves are melted. Brush lamb with apricot mixture occasionally during last 30 minutes of cooking.

4. Remove meat from oven and rest, loosely covered with foil, for 10 minutes. Using a sharp knife, slice between each rib bone and serve, allowing 2 ribs per serving.

¾ teaspoon garlic powder
¼ teaspoon salt
⅛ teaspoon black pepper
1 lamb rib roast (8-rib; about 2½ pounds)
¼ cup apricot preserves
2 teaspoons lemon juice

Easter Story Cookies

1   cup whole pecans
1   teaspoon vinegar
3   egg whites
⅛   teaspoon salt
1   cup sugar

Ever since the kids were little, we have made these cookies together the day before Easter. They are tasty, and baking them gives kids a wonderful reminder of the Easter story. We always decorate them with frosting on Easter morning in celebration.

MAKES 1 DOZEN COOKIES

1. Preheat oven at 300°F.

2. Place pecans in a zip lock bag. Let children beat them with a wooden spoon to break nuts into small pieces.
   (Explain that after Jesus was arrested, the Roman soldiers beat him. Read John 19:1–3.)

3. Let children smell the vinegar. Place vinegar into a mixing bowl.
   (Explain that when Jesus was thirsty on the cross He was given vinegar to drink. Read John 19:28–30.)

4. Add egg whites to vinegar.
   (Explain that eggs represent life. And that Jesus gave His life to give us life. Read John 10:10–11.)

5. Sprinkle a little salt into each child's hand. Let them taste it. Add salt to the bowl.
   (Explain that this represents the salty tears shed by Jesus' followers and the bitterness of our own sin. Read Luke 23:27.)

6. Add sugar to the bowl.
   (Explain that the sweetest part of the story is that Jesus died because He loves us. He wants us to know and belong to Him. Read PS. 34:8 and John 3:16.)

7. Beat eggs with an electric mixer until stiff peaks are formed.
   (*Explain that the color white represents the purity in God's eyes of those whose sins have been cleansed by Jesus. Read Isaac 1:18 and John 3:1–3.*)

8. Fold in nuts. Using a teaspoon, drop mixture onto a wax or parchment paper lined cookie sheet.
   (*Explain that each mound represents the rocky tomb where Jesus' body was laid. Read Matthew 27:57–60.*)

9. Place the cookie sheet in the oven, close the door and turn the oven off.

10. Give each child a piece of tape and seal the oven door.
    (*Explain that Jesus' tomb was sealed. Read Matthew 27:65–66.*)

11. Go to bed.
    (*Explain that they may feel sad to leave the cookies in the oven overnight. Jesus' followers were in despair when the tomb was sealed. Read John 16:20 and 22.*)

12. On Easter morning, open the oven and give everyone a cookie. Notice the cracked surface and take a bite. The cookies are hollow!
    (*On the first Easter Jesus' followers were amazed to find the tomb open and empty. Read Matthew 28:1–9.*)

He has risen, He has risen indeed!

America's Pride

Wild Card Chili

The Fourth of July is my birthday! I've always felt so lucky because the whole country celebrates with me. It was also my Grandma Edna's birthday. Our family partied with a BBQ and, of course, fireworks. It's still a family celebration—usually at Lake Tahoe with a day of boating, BBQ and fireworks.

SERVES 6

1. In a medium Dutch oven, brown beef with onions until meat is no longer pink. Pour off the fat. Add remaining ingredients, cover and simmer for 1 hour, stirring occasionally.

2. If desired, serve with grated cheese, sour cream and chopped onion.

1	pound ground beef
½	cup chopped onion
1	can (16 ounce) kidney beans
1	can (16 ounce) refried beans
1	can (8 ounce) tomato sauce
1	cup water
1	teaspoon chopped red bell peppers
½	teaspoon garlic salt
½	teaspoon salt
⅛	teaspoon black pepper
⅛	teaspoon cayenne pepper
3	tablespoons chili
1	tablespoon molasses

FOURTH OF JULY

Barbecued Beef Ribs

5 pounds beef short ribs
3 cups Black Jack Barbecue Sauce (see recipe below)

SERVES 4–6

1. Place ribs in a pan and pierce meat all over with a large fork. Pour sauce over ribs, turning to coat both sides. Marinate, refrigerated, for 8 hours, turning once.

2. Turn on broiler or prepare grill. Remove ribs from marinade and brush off excess to avoid burning. Broil or grill for 10 minutes; brush with marinade and cook another 5 minutes. Alternately, cook ribs, covered, in a 250°F oven for 1½ hours. Heat remaining sauce over medium heat until it boils, and serve with ribs.

Black Jack Barbecue Sauce

2 cups chopped onions
¼ cup minced hot chili peppers
6 cloves garlic, minced
1 cup strong black coffee
1 cup Worcestershire sauce
1 cup ketchup
½ cup cider vinegar
½ cup brown sugar
3 tablespoons chili powder
2 teaspoons salt

MAKES 5 CUPS

1. Combine all ingredients in a saucepan and simmer 25 minutes. Puree in a blender or food processor. Store refrigerated, up to 7 days.

Collector Recipe: Chocolate Zucchini Cake

Anyone who has planted zucchini knows that one plant produces more than a family can use. I started giving zucchini away to friends, but still I needed other ways to put my zucchini harvest to use, so I created this wonderfully moist and flavorful cake!

MAKES 1 CAKE

1. Combine margarine, oil, sugar, eggs, vanilla and milk in a large mixing bowl. Add flour, cocoa, baking powder, baking soda, spices and grated zucchini. Mix well.

2. Pour into greased Bundt pan. Bake at 350°F for 1 hour or until toothpick inserted in center comes out clean. Cool completely and drizzle with glaze (see recipe below).

½ cup margarine
½ cup vegetable oil
1¾ cups sugar
2 eggs
1 teaspoon vanilla
½ cup milk
2½ cups flour
4 tablespoons cocoa
½ teaspoon baking powder
1 teaspoon baking soda
½ teaspoon ground cinnamon
½ teaspoon ground cloves
2 cups grated zucchini

Glaze

1. Mix ingredients together until smooth and glossy. Drizzle over cake.

1 cup powdered sugar
1 tablespoon butter or margarine
1–2 tablespoons milk

Recipe and Memory by Karen Ford Carpenter

Crazy Cake

1½ cups all-purpose flour
3   tablespoons unsweetened cocoa
½   teaspoon salt
1   teaspoon baking soda
5   tablespoons vegetable oil
1   cup sugar
1   teaspoon vinegar
1   teaspoon vanilla
1   cup water
1   recipe Hershey's Cocoa Frosting
    (see recipe below)

This is my mom, Nancy Willey's, recipe—and it's the cake I'd always ask her to bake for my birthday. It has become a year round favorite of the Kinkade family.

SERVES 8

1. Preheat oven to 350°F. Butter and flour the bottom and sides of a 9-inch cake pan.

2. Sift together flour, cocoa, salt and baking soda and set aside. Using a mixer, combine oil, sugar, vinegar, vanilla and water. Add to dry ingredients and mix batter just until smooth.

3. Turn batter into prepared pan and bake 35 minutes, or until a toothpick inserted into the center comes out clean. The cake will double is size. Cool on a rack for 5 minutes, then invert onto a rack and complete cooling. Frost with Hershey's Cocoa Frosting.

NOTE: *For a large crowd, double the cake and frosting recipes and make a layer cake by stacking two layers together.*

Hershey's Cocoa Frosting

6   tablespoons butter, softened
½   cup Hershey's Cocoa
2⅔ cups powdered sugar, unsifted
1   teaspoon vanilla
⅓   cup milk

MAKES ENOUGH FOR 1 CAKE (9 INCH) OR 12 CUPCAKES

1. Using an electric mixer, cream butter with cocoa and sugar. Add vanilla and milk and mix to desired spreading consistency, adding additional milk, 1 tablespoon at a time, if necessary.

The Garden Party

The Blessings of Autumn

Country Fresh Biscuits

MAKES 24

3	cups all-purpose flour
¼	cup instant nonfat dry-milk powder
2	tablespoons double-acting baking powder
2	tablespoons sugar
1	teaspoon salt
1	teaspoon cream of tartar
1	cup shortening
1½	tablespoons water

1. Preheat oven to 400°F.

2. In large bowl using a fork, mix together all ingredients except shortening and water. With pastry blender or two knives used scissor-fashion, cut shortening into flour mixture until it resembles coarse crumbs. Stir in water until moistened. If mixture is dry, add more water, 1 tablespoon at a time.

3. Turn dough onto a floured work surface and, with floured hands, knead 8 to 10 times until smooth. With a floured rolling pin, roll dough ¾-inch thick. With a floured 2½-inch cookies cutter, cut biscuits and place onto a baking sheet, 1 inch apart. Press trimmings together, roll together and cut. Bake 20 to 25 minutes until golden brown. Serve warm.

NOTE: *Biscuits may be made in advance and stored in the freezer, uncooked, for up to 3 months. Cut biscuits and freeze on a baking sheet. When frozen, place biscuits into a freezer bag. To serve, place frozen biscuits onto a baking sheet and bake in a 400°F oven for 30 to 35 minutes until golden.*

THANKSGIVING

Microwave Cranberry Sauce

12 ounces fresh
    cranberries, rinsed
1¼ cups sugar
½ cup water
Grated zest of 1 orange

Cranberry sauce is delicious…and so easy! This is my sister Suzanne's recipe that we have shared since we started our families. She always brings it for Thanksgiving dinner.

SERVES 8

1. Combine ingredients into a microwave-safe pan. Cover tightly with plastic wrap and microwave on high for 5 minutes. Stir, replace plastic wrap and cook for an additional 5 minutes. Taste and add additional sugar, if necessary. Stir again and store, refrigerated, overnight. Sauce is best made one day in advance so flavors have time to meld together.

Campbell's Green Bean Casserole

1 can (10¾ ounce) Campbell's
    Cream of Mushroom Soup
    (or 98% Fat Free Cream of
    Mushroom Soup)
½ cup milk
Black pepper
4 cups cooked cut green beans
1 cup French's French Fried
    Onions

Thanksgiving just isn't Thanksgiving without Green Bean Casserole. As far as the Kinkade girls are concerned, this is one of our favorite parts of the meal.

SERVES 10

1. Preheat oven to 350°F.

2. In a medium casserole dish, mix soup, milk, pepper, green beans and ⅓ cup onions. Bake for 25 minutes. Stir and top with remaining onions. Bake 5 more minutes.

Autumn Lane

Fresh Apple Pie

¾ cup sugar
¼ cup all-purpose flour
½ teaspoon ground nutmeg
½ teaspoon ground cinnamon
⅛ teaspoon kosher salt
6 cups thinly sliced, peeled and cored tart apples (6–8 apples)
2 tablespoon butter, divided into pats
1 batch Standard Pie Crust (see recipe on opposite page)

*M*aking pies was thought to be an art in the Willey house. My sister Suzanne and I would spend hours in the kitchen with Mom perfecting a great pie crust. Mom wanted to be sure we could bake a delicious pie.

SERVES 10

1. Heat oven to 425°F.

2. In a bowl, mix together sugar, flour, nutmeg, cinnamon and salt. Add apples and mix thoroughly.

3. Pour into a 9-inch, crust-lined pie pan and dot with butter. Cover with second crust, seal and flute edges and cut ½-inch slits in the top for steam to escape. Cover outer edge of pie with a 3-inch wide strip of aluminum foil. Bake pie, removing foil for last 15 minutes of cooking, until crust is brown and juice begins to bubble through slits in crust, 40 to 50 minutes.

Standard Pie Crust

Makes 2 pie crusts (9-inches each) for 1 double-crust pie

1. In a bowl combine flour and salt. Using a pastry cutter or two knives, cut in shortening until particles are the size of small peas. Sprinkle in water, 1 tablespoon at a time, tossing with fork until all the flour is moistened and pastry almost cleans the sides of the bowl; add an additional 1 to 2 teaspoons water, if necessary.

2. Divide pastry in half and shape each half into a flattened round. Place one round on a lightly floured cloth-covered board and, using a floured or stocking covered rolling pin, roll out to an 11-inch diameter circle (2 inches larger than inverted pie plate). Fold pastry into quarters and place into pie pan. Unfold and press firmly against bottom and sides of pan. Add desired filing mixture.

3. Roll and fold second crust. Place over filling and unfold. Trim overhanging edge of pastry 1 inch from rim of plate. Fold and roll top edge under lower edge, pressing on rim to seal. Flute edge with fingers or a fork. Cover outer edge of pie with a 3-inch strip of aluminum foil to prevent excessive browning; remove foil during last 15 minutes of baking. Bake as directed in recipe.

⅔ cup plus 2 tablespoons shortening (or ⅔ cup lard)
2 cups all-purpose flour
1 teaspoon salt
4–5 tablespoons cold water

Travel
Memories

Thomas
Kinkade

Huevos Rancheros

8   corn tortillas
¼   cup oil
8   eggs
1   cup shredded cheddar cheese
1   can black beans
1   jar favorite salsa (optional)
1   recipe Rancheros Sauce
    (see recipe below)
Salt
Black pepper

Thom loves to make this recipe for the family (so you know it must be pretty easy)! These Mexican eggs have become a favorite Kinkade family brunch.

SERVES 4

1. Heat a small skillet until hot. Warm the tortillas until crisp and light brown, about 1 minute per each side. Keep tortillas warm.

2. Heat 2 tablespoons oil in a large skillet until hot. Break eggs into a measuring cup; carefully slip 4 eggs, 1 at a time, into skillet. Immediately reduce heat. Cook slowly, spooning oil onto eggs until whites are set and the yolks begin to set. Season with salt and pepper. Repeat with remaining eggs.

3. To serve, spread 2 tablespoons black beans and spoon 1 tablespoon of salsa and/or the Rancheros Sauce over each tortilla and top each with 1 egg. Spoon additional sauce over eggs and top with cheese. If desired, serve with salsa.

Rancheros Sauce

1   tablespoon vegetable oil
1   medium onion, chopped
½   green bell pepper, seeded
    and chopped
1   clove garlic, minced
2   cups chopped ripe tomatoes
    (or 1 can (16 ounce) diced
    tomatoes, undrained)
¼   cup chopped green chilies
8   drops red pepper sauce
½   teaspoon sugar
⅛   teaspoon salt

MAKES 2 CUPS

1. In a skillet over medium heat, add oil and cook onion, green bell pepper and garlic until tender, about 5 minutes. Stir in remaining ingredients and bring to a boil; reduce heat. Simmer, uncovered until slightly thickened, about 15 minutes.

Puerto Vallarta Beach

Island Afternoon, Greece

Athenian Salad

SERVES 8

1. Tear lettuce and romaine into bite-sized pieces. Place lettuce, romaine, radishes, cucumber and green onions into a large plastic bag. Seal bag and refrigerate. In a small airtight container, combine vinegar, salt and oregano. Cover and refrigerate.

2. To serve, shake dressing to combine. Add contents of bag into a large bowl; add olives and dressing and toss. Top with cheese and, if using, anchovies.

1	medium head leafy green lettuce
1	head romaine lettuce
10	radishes, sliced
1	medium cucumber, sliced
6	green onions, sliced
½	cup olive oil
⅓	cup red wine vinegar
1	teaspoon salt
1	teaspoon dried oregano leaves
24	Greek olives
¼	cup crumbled feta cheese
1	can (2 ounce) rolled anchovies with capers, drained (optional)

Coney Island Clam Chowder

1 pound fresh or canned clams, steam and discard shells and reserve liquor

4 tablespoons rendered bacon fat, butter or vegetable oil

2 onions, chopped

1 clove garlic, minced

1 bell pepper, seeded and diced

Leaves from 3 stalks of celery, chopped

1 tablespoon chopped fresh parsley

¼ teaspoon curry powder

½ quart solid pack tomatoes

1 quart clam juice

1 quart water

1 potato, diced

½ teaspoon black pepper

Salt

This recipe is from a favorite San Francisco restaurant, the Tadich Grill.

SERVES 6

1. Chop the clam meat roughly and set aside.

2. In a large stockpot, heat the bacon fat, butter or oil. Add the onions, garlic, bell pepper, celery leaves, parsley and curry powder and sauté until vegetables start to brown. Add the tomatoes, potatoes, clam juice and the reserved clam liquor added to enough water to yield 1 quart. Simmer for 90 minutes. Add the chopped clams, season with salt and pepper and simmer for an additional 20 minutes.

New York, Snow on Seventh Avenue, 1932

Pike Place Market, Seattle

Butternut Squash and White Bean Soup

It's a happy thing that squash is plentiful in Fall and Winter; this soup is a great winter warm-up. It's also one of Thom's all-time favorite recipes.

SERVES 8

1. In a large Dutch oven over medium heat, add oil, onion, garlic, cumin and cinnamon and cook for 5 minutes, or until onion is tender, but not browned. Add squash, pepper, broth and tomatoes and bring to a boil. Reduce heat, cover and simmer for about 30 minutes or until squash is tender.

2. In a blender or food processor, puree the soup, in batches, if necessary. For a chunkier soup, only puree half. Return soup to the pan, add beans and cook over medium heat for 5 minutes, until heated through. Season with salt and pepper.

3. Serve with grated cheese and sourdough bread.

1 tablespoon olive oil
1 cup chopped onion
4 cloves garlic, minced
½ teaspoon ground cumin
¾ teaspoon ground cinnamon
3 cups peeled, seeded and diced butternut squash (about 1½ pounds)
⅛ teaspoon black pepper
3 cups vegetable broth
1 can (14½ ounce) whole tomatoes, with liquid
1 can (14½ ounce) diced tomatoes, with liquid
1 can (16 ounce) cannellini beans, drained
Salt
Grated Vella dry Jack cheese
Sourdough bread

Vegetable Beef Soup

3 pounds beef short ribs
3 quarts beef broth or water
¼ teaspoon black pepper, plus
more for seasoning
1 onion, chopped
1 cup chopped celery
1 cup chopped carrots
1 cup sliced cabbage
1 cup diced potatoes
⅓ cup barley
3½ cups canned diced
tomatoes, drained
2 teaspoon dried parsley
1 can green beans, diced
Salt

*T*his Kinkade family original recipe came from my mom, Nancy Willey's kitchen. Made from whatever you have on hand—or what's coming in from the garden.

MAKES 8 QUARTS

1. Season short ribs with pepper and place in a large stockpot. Add broth or water and simmer, covered, over low heat for 3 hours. Remove meat, separate from bones, pull into bite-sized pieces and refrigerate. Refrigerate stock in stockpot overnight.

2. Remove fat layer from top of chilled stock and discard. Place pot over medium heat and bring to a boil, reduce heat, add barley and cook for 15 minutes. Add remaining ingredients and reserved beef and cook for an additional 10 minutes. Season with salt and pepper.

Chicago, Winter at the Water Tower

Biarritz

French Mushroom Soup

SERVES 4

1. Preheat oven to 400°F.

2. In a saucepan over medium heat, melt butter and cook onions for 5 minutes. Add mushrooms and cook, stirring constantly, for 3 minutes. Remove and reserve few mushroom slices for garnish. Add broth and vinegar and bring to boil. Reduce heat, cover and simmer for 10 minutes. Puree half of the soup in a blender and return to pot.

3. Place bread onto a baking sheet and toast in the oven until slightly browned, about 10 minutes. Remove toast and heat broiler. Divide soup equally into 4 oven-proof bowls. Top each serving with 1 toast slice, ¼ cup shredded cheese, reserved mushroom slices and 1 tablespoon Parmesan cheese. Broil for 3 to 5 minutes until golden brown.

3 tablespoons butter
2½ cups sliced onions
¾ pound mushrooms, sliced
2 cans (14½ ounces each) beef broth
2 tablespoons white vinegar
4 slices baguette, ½-inch thick
1 cup shredded Swiss or Gruyere cheese (about 4 ounces)
¼ cup grated Parmesan cheese

Irish Stew

2 pounds boneless lamb shoulder, fat trimmed and cut into 1-inch pieces

6 medium potatoes (about 2 pounds), cut into ½-inch dice

3 medium onions, sliced

2 cups water

2 teaspoons salt

¼ teaspoon black pepper

¼ cup chopped fresh parsley

SERVES 6

1. In a large Dutch oven over medium heat, combine lamb, potatoes, onions and water and season with salt and pepper. Add water. Bring to a boil, reduce heat and cover. Simmer until lamb is tender, 1½ to 2 hours. Skim fat from broth (see Note below). Sprinkle with parsley. Serve in bowls with pickled red cabbage, if desired.

NOTE: *To remove fat easily, prepare stew the day before, cover and refrigerate. Remove fat layer from top before reheating.*

Collector Recipe: Irish Potato Soup

½ cup unsalted butter

1 medium onion, thinly sliced and diced

3 leeks (white and green part), thinly sliced

3 large potatoes, peeled and cut into thin slices

5½ cups chicken broth

1 teaspoon sea salt

¼ teaspoon ground black pepper

Toppings: shredded cheddar cheese, crumbled cooked bacon, sour cream (optional)

My husband and I have been married for many years and this is the first meal I prepared that he really loved! Not only do I make it on St. Patrick's Day every year, but it also makes for a hearty meal on a chilly, winter day!

MAKES ABOUT 3 QUARTS

1. Melt butter in a large saucepan over low heat, and stir in onion and leek. Cover and cook 20 minutes. Stir in potato. Cover and cook 15 minutes. Stir in broth, salt and pepper; bring to a boil. Reduce heat and simmer for 30 minutes or until potato is tender.

2. Remove from heat and cool slightly. Mix soup with a hand mixer in a saucepan until smooth, making sure to scrape down sides. Cook over medium heat until thoroughly heated. Serve with suggested toppings as desired.

Recipe and Memory by Lezlie Cohn-Oswald

Blossom Bridge

Antigua Sunset

Chili Verde

SERVES 10

1. Set a slow cooker to low heat.

2. Heat a large skillet over medium heat and add 2 tablespoons oil. Season beef with salt and pepper and brown, stirring frequently. Transfer meat into a slow cooker.

3. Return skillet to heat and add remaining 2 tablespoons oil. Cook the onions and garlic in skillet until softened. Add tomatoes with their liquid and season with salt. Add tomatillos, chilies, parsley or cilantro, lemon or lime juice, oregano, cumin, coriander and allspice. Pour into slow cooker with beef and stir. Cover and cook 7 hours or until tender. Adjust seasonings as desired. If desired, serve with sour cream and warm tortillas.

¼ cup vegetable oil, divided

2½ pounds boneless chuck, cut into 1-inch cubes

2 onions, finely chopped

2 cloves garlic, minced

2 cans (14½ ounces each) crushed tomatoes, with liquid

1 can (12 ounce) tomatillos (whole green Latin tomatoes), drained and coarsely chopped

1 can (4 ounce) diced mild green chilies

1 cup chopped fresh parsley or cilantro

⅓ cup freshly squeezed lemon or lime juice

2 teaspoons dried oregano

1½ teaspoons ground cumin

1 teaspoon ground coriander

⅛ teaspoon ground allspice

Salt

Black pepper

Rice with Black Beans

1 tablespoon vegetable oil
1 medium onion, chopped
1 can (14½ ounce) tomatoes
1 can (16 ounce) black beans,
  with liquid
½ teaspoon dried oregano leaves
½ teaspoon garlic powder
1½ cups instant brown rice

Rice with black beans—simple, satisfying—and, for me, something more. I love this recipe because it came from my sister Suzanne, and preparing it reminds me of our fun times together!

SERVES 8

1. In a medium pot, heat oil over medium heat. Add the onions and, stirring frequently, cook until translucent but not brown. Add tomatoes, beans, oregano and garlic powder. Bring to boil.

2. Add rice and stir. Return to boil then reduce heat, cover and simmer for 5 minutes. Remove from heat. Let stand 5 minutes and then fluff with a spoon.

Sedona Cliffs

The Old Mission, Santa Barbara

Crocked Pork and Beans

SERVES 8

1. Soak beans in water overnight.

2. Set a slow cooker to low heat.

3. Heat a large skillet over medium heat and brown the meat. Remove meat from pan and set aside. Return skillet to heat and lightly brown the onion and garlic in meat drippings. Blend in tomato paste, brown sugar, molasses, soy sauce, mustard, pepper, salt and beer. Remove from heat.

4. Add half of the sauce and beans, add in the meat and cover with remaining sauce and beans. Cover and cook for 10 hours or until tender. Stir before serving, breaking meat into chunks.

1	pound dried great northern or other white beans
1	pound boneless pork shoulder, in one piece
1	onion, minced
1	clove garlic, minced
½	cup tomato paste
½	cup brown sugar
1	tablespoon molasses
2	teaspoons soy sauce
1	teaspoon dry mustard
⅛	teaspoon black pepper
2	teaspoons salt
1	bottle of beer (about 12 ounces)

Garbanzos Italienne

⅓ cup red wine vinegar
1 teaspoon sugar
¼ teaspoon oregano
1 teaspoon salt
¼ cup extra virgin olive oil
3 tablespoons chopped onion
1 clove garlic, minced
1 can (15 ounce) garbanzo beans, drained and rinsed
1 can (15 ounce) kidneys beans, drained and rinsed
1 can (15 ounce) green beans, drained and rinsed
Black pepper

Good is good. My girls love this just like my sister and I did when my mother used to keep a big bowl of it in the refrigerator. We serve it straight or mix it with other salads.

SERVES 8

1. In a large bowl, whisk together vinegar, sugar, oregano, salt and pepper until sugar and salt have dissolved. Whisk in oil. Add remaining ingredients and mix thoroughly. Cover and refrigerate overnight.

2. Beans are best made one day in advance so flavors have time to meld together.

Venice Canal

Golden Gate Bridge, San Francisco

Italian Meatballs

Serves 6

1. Bring a large pot of salted water to a boil.

2. In a bowl, combine all of the ingredients except marinara sauce and mix well. Form into small meatballs. Add to boiling water and cook until they float to top of the pan. Drain and add to marinara sauce.

1½	pounds ground beef
2	tablespoons dried onions
1	teaspoon garlic salt
1	teaspoon dried sage
¼	cup chopped fresh parsley
2	slices bread, soaked in milk
6	cups favorite marinara sauce, heated

Kinkade Family Favorite Pasta

3 tablespoons olive oil

3 cloves garlic, minced

1 pound mushrooms, sliced

1 bunch green onions, chopped

1¼ pounds prawns, deveined

1 cup chicken broth

2 packages (9 ounces each) fresh fettuccini, cooked according to package instructions

½ cup prepared pesto (or Blender Pesto recipe on page 114)

8 cups baby spinach leaves (about 10 ounces)

Grated Parmesan cheese

I hope your family enjoys this recipe as much as ours does. We all love this Kinkade family classic—and you can put Thom at the head of the list!

SERVES 8

1. In a large skillet over medium heat, add oil and garlic and cook until garlic begins to brown, about 2 minutes. Add mushrooms and onions and cook until softened, about 4 minutes. Add shrimp and cook for 2 minutes, until shrimp have turned pink but are still slightly undercooked. Add broth and simmer, then add pesto. Toss with pasta and serve on a bed of spinach leaves.

2. Serve with grated Parmesan cheese.

Venice

Hotel del Coronado

Pasta Shells Florentine

SERVES 4

1. Heat oven to 375°F.

2. In a bowl, combine spinach, mozzarella cheese, cottage cheese, egg white, Parmesan cheese and nutmeg. Fill each shell with a heaping scoop of spinach mixture and place stuffed shells into a baking dish. Spoon sauce over shells, cover with foil and bake for 25 minutes. Remove foil and bake for another 10 minutes. Serve with Parmesan cheese.

1 package (10 ounce) frozen chopped spinach, thawed and well drained
1 cup part-skim mozzarella cheese (about 4 ounces)
1 cup nonfat cottage cheese
1 egg white
1 tablespoon grated Parmesan cheese, plus extra for serving
¼ teaspoon ground nutmeg
16 jumbo pasta shells, cooked according to package instruction and drained
1 jar (13½ ounce) favorite spaghetti sauce

Pasta with Basil and Cheese Sauce

10   ounces spaghetti or
      other noodles
⅔   cup packed basil
      leaves, chopped
⅓   cup grated Parmesan cheese,
      plus extra for serving
⅓   cup oil olive
2   tablespoons pine nuts
      or walnuts
½   teaspoon salt
⅛   teaspoon black pepper
1   clove garlic
2   tablespoons butter

SERVES 6

1. In a large pot of boiling salted water, cook pasta according to package instructions.

2. While pasta is cooking, place all remaining ingredients except butter in a blender and blend until mixture is a uniform consistency.

3. Drain pasta and toss with the basil mixture and the butter. Serve with additional Parmesan cheese, if desired.

Portofino

Chinatown, San Francisco

Asian Beef Noodles

SERVES 6

1. Heat a wok or large skillet over medium heat until hot. Add 1 teaspoon vegetable oil and stir fry half of the beef for 3 to 4 minutes, stirring the meat constantly with a heat resistant spatula. Remove beef and repeat with remaining oil and beef. Set cooked meat aside.

2. Return pan to heat, add garlic and ginger and cook for 30 seconds. Add water and bring to a boil. Add noodles, broccoli, carrots and seasoning packets from ramen noodles. Return to a boil then reduce heat. Simmer for 3 minutes or until noodles are tender and most of the liquid is absorbed. Return beef to pan, mix to combine and heat through. Garnish with green onions.

1   pound lean boneless beef top round, cut into ¼-inch strips
2   teaspoons vegetable oil, divided
3   cloves garlic, minced
1   piece (1 inch) fresh ginger, peeled and grated
2   cups water
2   packages (3 ounces each) beef flavored ramen noodles, broken into large pieces
3   cups broccoli florets
2   carrots, sliced
2   green onions, sliced

Asparagus Tomato Quiche

4   large eggs
3   tablespoons all-purpose flour
1   teaspoon paprika
1   teaspoon salt
½   teaspoon dry mustard
1½   cups half-and-half
2   cups grated Swiss cheese
10   fresh asparagus spears, washed and trimmed
1   frozen prepared pie crust (10 inch), thawed and partially baked
1   medium tomato, sliced into four ¼-inch slices

SERVES 6

1. Preheat oven to 375°F.

2. In a bowl, beat together eggs, flour, paprika, mustard and salt; stir in cheese. Reserve 6 asparagus spears for the top. Chop remaining asparagus into 1-inch lengths and lay into pie shell. Pour in egg mixture and bake 20 minutes. Remove and quickly arrange tomato and reserved asparagus on top in a wagon wheel pattern. Bake for another 25 minutes, until mixture sets and top starts to brown.

Brussels

Boston

Kennedy Quiche

SERVES 8

1. Preheat oven to 325°F.

2. In a bowl, combine cheese, melted butter, flour, mustard and ½ teaspoon salt and press into the bottom of a 9-inch pie pan. Bake for 20 minutes until it browns slightly. Remove from oven and increase temperature to 400°F.

3. In a pot over medium heat, combine milk, half-and-half and onion and bring to a boil. Lower heat and simmer for 3 minutes. Remove from heat and cool. Add eggs, spinach, 1 teaspoon salt and pepper and mix thoroughly. Pour filling into prepared crust and bake for 15 minutes, until filling sets and top begins to brown.

1½ cups grated cheddar cheese
½ cup butter, melted
¾ cup all-purpose flour
¼ teaspoon dried mustard
1½ teaspoons salt, divided
½ cup milk
½ cup half-and-half
¼ cup chopped onion
⅛ teaspoon black pepper
3 eggs
1 cup frozen chopped spinach, thawed and drained

Austrian Ham and Noodle Casserole

8 ounces uncooked wide
    egg noodles
¼ cup butter
1 medium onion, chopped
1 egg, beaten
½ cup plain yogurt
2 cups diced cooked smoked
   ham (about ½ pound)
½ teaspoon caraway seed
   (optional)
¼ teaspoon black pepper
¼ cup bread crumbs
½ teaspoon paprika

When Thom was at Art School, he became fast friends with fellow artist Jim Gurney; our families still enjoy getting together today! This recipe comes from Jim's wife, Jeanette Gurney; for us, it's a delicious taste of our good old days together.

SERVES 4

1. Preheat oven to 375°F.

2. In a large pot of salted boiling water, cook noodles for 3 minutes. Cover pot and remove from heat; let stand 10 minutes; drain and return noodles to pot. Add butter and onion to noodles and stir.

3. In a large bowl, combine egg and yogurt; add ham, caraway seeds, pepper and noodle mixture and mix thoroughly.

4. Sprinkle bread crumbs evenly in greased casserole. Pour mixture on top of bread crumbs and top with paprika. Cook, uncovered until mixture is set, 40 to 45 minutes.

Heiligen Blut

Plaza Lights, Kansas City

Shredded Potatoes & Ham Pie

SERVES 6

1. Preheat oven to 350°F.

2. In a bowl combine eggs, vegetables, ham, 1 cup cheese, milk and onion. Set aside. Combine potatoes and ½ cup cheese and press onto the bottom of 9-inch pie plate. Top with vegetable and ham mixture and bake for 45 to 50 minutes or till center is set. Allow to stand 5 to 10 minutes before serving.

NOTE: *Try substituting shredded beef or chicken for the ham.*

4   eggs, beaten
1   cup frozen mixed peas and carrots, thawed
1   cup chopped cooked ham
1½ cups shredded cheddar cheese, divided
½   cup milk
¼   teaspoon minced dried onion
2   medium potatoes, peeled and shredded (about 2 cups)

Chicken Pot Pie

PASTRY:

1½ cups all-purpose flour

1 teaspoon salt

⅓ cup chilled butter, cut into pieces

1 large egg

2–3 tablespoons ice water

FILLING:

4 cups diced cooked chicken

1 tablespoon butter

1 pound fresh mushrooms, sliced

¼ cup dry white wine or water

1½ cups whipping cream

2 tablespoons all-purpose flour

1½ teaspoons paprika

½ teaspoon salt

½ teaspoon black pepper

¾ cup reduced-sodium chicken broth

GLAZE:

1 large egg, lightly beaten

This recipe takes me back to my roots in the old country. It comes from my German grandmother, Louise Ferris, who learned it from her mother.

SERVES 6

1. Prepare the pastry: in a medium bowl, mix together flour and salt. Using a pastry knife or two knives, cut butter into flour until coarse crumbs form. In a small bowl, beat together egg and water. Add to the flour mixture; mix lightly until a soft dough forms. Shape into a disk, wrap in plastic wrap and chill in the refrigerator for 1 hour.

2. Prepare the filling: place chicken in a pie pan or 2-quart casserole dish. In a large skillet, melt butter over low heat. Add mushrooms, increase the heat to medium-high and cook until browned and the liquid evaporates, about 2 minutes. Add mushroom mixture to chicken; stir to combine.

3. In a medium saucepan, whisk together cream, flour, paprika, salt and pepper. Cook over low heat until thickened, about 5 minutes. Whisk in broth. Pour sauce over chicken mixture.

4. Preheat oven to 400°F.

5. On a lightly floured surface, using a lightly floured rolling pin, roll the pastry to fit the top of the casserole. Place dough on top of filling and trim and seal the edges. Roll out trimmings. Cut out leaves. Brush pastry with glaze; add the decorations and brush again with glaze.

6. Bake until filling is bubbly and crust is browned, 25 to 30 minutes. Transfer to a wire rack to cool slightly. Serve warm.

Solvang

Piccadilly Circus, London

Cornish Hens with Wild Rice

Serves 4

1. Preheat oven to 325°F.

2. Place rice and water into a pot over medium heat and bring to a boil. Reduce heat, cover and simmer for 12 minutes, or until water is absorbed. Fluff rice and spread evenly into a baking dish.

3. In a pan over medium heat, melt 2 tablespoons butter. Add onion and cook until translucent but not brown. Sprinkle in flour and stir. Add broth; bring to a boil and then stir in peas. Remove from heat and pour over rice.

4. Rub the hens with remaining 2 tablespoons butter, mustard, salt and pepper. Arrange on rice mixture, skin side up and cover with foil and bake for 45 minutes, until rice is done and hens are tender.

1	package (6 ounce) wild rice
1¼	cups water
4	tablespoons (½ stick) butter, divided
1	medium onion, finely chopped
1	tablespoon all-purpose flour
2	cups chicken broth
1	package (10 ounce) frozen green peas, thawed
2	cornish hens, halved
⅛	teaspoon dry mustard
Black pepper	
Salt	

Sicilian Skillet Chicken

6   tablespoons grated Parmesan
     cheese, divided
3   tablespoons all-purpose flour
4   half boneless, skinless chicken
     cutlets (2 whole breasts),
     pounded slightly
2   tablespoons olive oil
1   cup sliced mushrooms
1   green bell pepper,
     seeded and diced
½   onion, finely chopped
½   teaspoon dried basil
1   can (14½ ounce)
     crushed tomatoes
Salt
Black pepper

SERVES 4

1. In a shallow dish, combine 3 tablespoons cheese, flour, salt and pepper.

2. Heat a skillet over medium heat and add oil. Dredge chicken into cheese and flour mixture and then place directly into hot pan. Cook for 4 minutes, flip and cook for another 4 minutes or until chicken is cooked thoroughly. Remove to a serving dish and keep warm.

3. Return skillet to heat and add mushrooms, bell pepper, onion and basil; cook until soft. Add tomatoes and cook, uncovered, until thickened, about 8 to 10 minutes. Spoon sauce over chicken and top with remaining cheese. Serve with your favorite pasta.

Fish with Sour Cream (Betyar Fogas)

SERVES 4

1. Preheat oven to 350°F.

2. Rinse and pat fish dry with paper towels. Arrange fillets in a baking dish.

3. In a skillet, heat butter and add mushrooms and onions. Cook, stirring, until mushrooms brown, about 4 minutes. Spoon mushrooms mixture over fish and season with salt and pepper.

4. Combine sour cream and cheese and spread over mushroom mixture. Sprinkle with bread crumbs. Cook, uncovered, until fish flakes easily with fork, 25 to 30 minutes. Garnish with paprika and parsley.

1 pound fish fillets
1 tablespoon butter
1 cup sliced mushrooms
1 small onion, chopped
½ teaspoon salt
⅛ teaspoon black pepper
½ cup sour cream
3 tablespoons grated Parmesan cheese
2 tablespoons bread crumbs
½ teaspoon paprika
2 tablespoons chopped fresh parsley

Newport Harbor

Sunset over Riga

Beef Stroganov

SERVES 4

1. Using a sharp knife, cut beef across the grain into strips, 1½ x ½ inch. For easier cutting, partially freeze beef for about 1½ hours.

2. Heat 2 tablespoons butter in a large skillet. Add mushrooms, onions and garlic. Cover and simmer, stirring occasionally, until onions are tender, 5 to 10 minutes. Remove vegetables and any liquid from skillet and reserve.

3. Return skillet to heat and add remaining 2 tablespoons butter. Add beef and cook over medium heat until brown, about 5 minutes, Add water, bouillon, salt and pepper. Bring to a boil then reduce heat. Cover and simmer until beef is cooked as desired, 10 minutes. Add vegetable mixture and simmer to warm through; stir in sour cream and mustard and cook for 1 minute. Remove from heat and top with parsley. If desired, serve over noodles or rice.

1	pound boneless beef sirloin or top loin steak, ½-inch thick
4	tablespoons butter, divided
8	ounces mushrooms, sliced
2	medium onions, sliced
1	clove garlic, minced
½	cup water
1	teaspoon instant beef bouillon
1	teaspoon salt
¼	teaspoon black pepper
1	cup sour cream
½	teaspoon prepared mustard
2	tablespoons chopped fresh parsley

Goulash

1   tablespoon vegetable oil
1   pound ground beef
1   onion, chopped
1   clove garlic
½   bell pepper, seeded and diced
1   tablespoon chili powder
1   can (28 ounce) tomatoes
1   can (8 ounce) tomato sauce
1   can (16 ounce) kidney beans

This hearty classic is another that comes from Grandma Louise, my German grandmother. She was simply a great cook!

SERVES 4

1. In a large skillet, heat the oil and brown the meat with the onions, about 5 minutes. Add garlic, pepper and chili powder and cook for 3 more minutes. Add remaining ingredients and simmer for 30 minutes, stirring occasionally.

2. If desired, serve over prepared macaroni

Luxembourg Gardens

Paris, City of Lights

Coq au Vin Rosettes

SERVES **8**

1. Preheat oven to 325°F.

2. In a skillet, melt butter over medium-high heat. Add mushrooms and onion and cook for 5 minutes or until tender, stirring occasionally. Add chicken, wine, tarragon, white pepper and salt. Bring to a boil and reduce heat. Simmer, covered, for 5 minutes, stirring once. Remove from heat.

3. Halve each lasagna noodle lengthwise. Curl each noodle in a 2½-inch-diameter ring and place, cut side down, in a baking dish. Using a slotted spoon, spoon chicken mixture into center of lasagna rings, reserving liquid in skillet.

4. Add the cream cheese to reserved liquid and heat, stirring, until cream cheese is melted. Reduce heat and stir in sour cream, flour and half-and-half. Cook, stirring frequently, over medium heat until sauce thickens; spoon over stuffed rings. If desired, top with slivered almonds. Bake, covered, for 35 minutes or until heated through.

NOTE: *For a lower-fat version, use reduced-fat cream cheese, light sour cream and milk in place of regular cream cheese, regular sour cream and half-and-half.*

2	tablespoons butter
3	cups sliced mushrooms (about 8 ounces)
½	cup chopped onion
8	boneless, skinless chicken cutlets (from 4 whole breasts), cut into 1-inch pieces
¾	cup dry white wine
½	teaspoon dried tarragon, crushed
⅛	teaspoon white pepper
⅛	teaspoon salt
8	lasagna noodles, cooked according to package instructions
1	package (8 ounce) cream cheese, diced
½	cup sour cream
2	tablespoons all-purpose flour
½	cup half-and-half, light cream or milk
1	cup shredded Gruyere cheese (about 4 ounces)
1	cup shredded Muenster cheese (about 4 ounces)
¼	cup slivered almonds, toasted (optional)

French Farmhouse Garlic Chicken

4	boneless, skinless chicken cutlets, from 2 whole breasts
¼	teaspoon salt
¼	teaspoon black pepper
1	tablespoon vegetable oil
40	cloves garlic, unpeeled
½	cup dry white wine
½	cup plus 2 tablespoons chicken broth
1	tablespoon freshly squeezed lemon juice
1	teaspoon dried basil, crushed
½	teaspoon dried oregano, crushed
4	teaspoons all-purpose flour

SERVES 4

1. Rinse chicken, pat dry with paper towels and season with salt and pepper. In a large skillet over medium-high heat, add oil, then add chicken and garlic cloves. Cook chicken for 2 to 3 minutes on each side until brown. Slowly add the wine, ½ cup broth, lemon juice, basil and oregano. Cover and simmer for 6 to 8 minutes, or until chicken is tender and no longer pink. Using a slotted spoon, transfer chicken and garlic to a warm serving platter; keep warm.

2. In a small bowl, stir together the flour and the 2 tablespoons broth. Stir into pan juices. Bring to boiling. Cook and stir for 1 minute more. Spoon sauce over chicken. If desired, serve with mashed potatoes or rice.

NOTE: *If you prefer, peel the garlic before cooking. Use the flat side of a large knife to mash them slightly and then peel off the skins.*

Charleston, Sunset on Rainbow Row

Paris, Eiffel Tower

Coquilles St. Jacques

SERVES 4

1. In a stockpot over medium heat, place the onion, celery, bay leaf, lemon, water and a good pinch of salt and pepper. Bring to a boil and simmer for 10 minutes. Reduce heat, add the white wine and scallops and simmer for 5 to 10 minutes, depending on the size of the scallops, until just cooked. Scallops are done when creamy colored all the way through. Remove immediately, reserving cooking liquid and keep warm. Increase temperature to high and reduce cooking liquid to 1 cup.

2. Cook the mushrooms in 1 tablespoon butter without letting them get too brown. Set aside.

3. Melt the remaining 4 tablespoons butter, add flour and cook until frothy. Gradually add the scallop liquid, stirring until smooth and bubbly. Beat the egg yolks with the cream and slowly beat the egg mixture into the sauce. Add the mushrooms, scallops, lemon juice and season with salt and pepper. If desired, cook to this point up to one day in advance.

4. Heat broiler. Place the scallops in a single layer in a baking dish or individual dishes or scallop shells. Spoon sauce over the top and broil, until heated through and flecked with brown. If desired, pipe or spoon a border of mashed potatoes around the dish before broiling.

1	small onion
1	stalk celery
1	bay leaf
1	slice lemon
2	cups water
½	cup dry white wine
1	pound scallops
8	fresh mushrooms
5	tablespoons butter
3	tablespoons all-purpose flour
2	egg yolks
1	cup cream
1	teaspoon freshly squeezed lemon juice

Pinch of salt and black pepper

Asparagus Beef

1 pound flank steak, sliced
   against the grain into
   ¼-inch-thick slices
2 tablespoons vegetable oil
2 pounds asparagus, sliced on
   the diagonal into 1-inch pieces
1 cup water, divided
1 tablespoon Asian black
   bean paste
½ teaspoon cornstarch
½ cup water

SERVES 4

1. Heat 1 tablespoon oil in a wok or skillet over high heat. Add asparagus and toss continuously for 2 minutes. Lower heat, add ½ cup water, cover pan and cook for about 3 minutes. Remove the asparagus and set aside.

2. Return pan to high heat and add remaining 1 tablespoon oil. Add the beef and black bean sauce. Cook, stirring constantly, for about 4 minutes; add asparagus and continue cooking for 1 minute. Mix the cornstarch with remaining ½ cup water, add to the pan and cook until sauce thickens, about 1 minute. If desired, serve with rice

Venetian Anchovy Pasta

1–2 packages dried fettuccini or
   spaghetti (enough for 4)
6 salt-packed anchovies
Several sprigs Italian parsley
5–6 cloves garlic
½–¾ cup virgin olive oil
¾ cup shredded
   Parmesan cheese
Freshly ground black pepper
   to taste
Lemon wedges (optional)

Talk about an image and a recipe being linked in your mind! Thom was painting the image of the Grand Canal in Venice that you see on page 57, when he took a lunch break, then returned to finish it. This is the meal he enjoyed that day; every time I fix this recipe, it brings us back to that wonderful Venetian adventure.

SERVES 4

1. Rinse and fillet the anchovies. Cut two anchovies into thin strips and set aside for garnish. Finely chop the remaining anchovies. Mince some Italian parsley, about 4 to 5 tablespoons. Peel and chop the garlic.

2. Cook pasta according to package directions and when it is nearly done, in a separate pan over low heat, add oil and garlic. Let the garlic sizzle gently about a minute, but don't let it get brown. When the aroma starts to fill the room, remove the pan from the flame and add the chopped anchovies. Stir anchovies into the garlic-oil, then add the drained pasta and parley. Toss well and add some coarsely ground black pepper over top.

3. Serve immediately in hot dishes. Garnish with the reserved strips of anchovy and sprinkle Parmesan cheese over top. You may also top with a wedge of lemon, if desired.

A View from Cannery Row, Monterey

Fish Fillets with Spinach

SERVES 4

1. Preheat oven to 350°F.

2. Rinse and pat fish dry with paper towels and set aside.

3. In a skillet, heat butter over low heat until melted. Stir in flour, bouillon, cayenne and white pepper. Cook over low heat, stirring constantly, until mixture is smooth and bubbly. Stir in milk. Heat to boiling and cook for 1 minute. Add cheese and cook, stirring constantly, just until cheese melts; remove from heat.

4. Place spinach in a baking dish and sprinkle with lemon juice. Arrange fish on spinach and season with salt. Spread sauce over fish and spinach. Cook, uncovered, until fish flakes easily with fork, 20 to 25 minutes. To serve, sprinkle with Parmesan cheese and paprika.

2	tablespoons butter
2	tablespoons all-purpose flour
1	teaspoon instant chicken bouillon
⅛	teaspoon cayenne pepper
⅛	teaspoon white pepper
1	cup milk
⅔	cup shredded Swiss or cheddar cheese
1	package (10 ounce) frozen chopped spinach, thawed and well drained
1	tablespoon freshly squeezed lemon juice
1	pound fish fillets
½	teaspoon salt
2	tablespoons grated Parmesan cheese
½	teaspoon paprika

Irish Soda Bread

4½ cups all-purpose flour
3   tablespoons sugar
1   tablespoon double-acting
     baking powder
1   teaspoon salt
1   teaspoon baking soda
6   tablespoons butter
2   eggs
1½ cups buttermilk

MAKES 1 LOAF

1. Preheat oven to 350°F. Grease a round casserole dish.

2. In large bowl with fork, mix flour, sugar, baking powder, salt and baking soda. With pastry blender or two knives used scissor-fashion, cut in butter until mixture resembles coarse crumbs.

3. Beat eggs. Remove 1 tablespoon and reserve. Stir buttermilk and remaining egg into flour mixture, just until flour is moistened. Dough will be sticky. Turn dough into well-floured surface. With floured hands, knead about 10 times to mix thoroughly. Shape dough into a ball and place in casserole. In center of ball, with sharp knife, cut a 4-inch cross, about ¼-inch deep. Brush dough with reserved egg.

4. Bake bread for 1 hour and 10 minutes or until toothpick inserted in center of loaf comes out clean. Cool in casserole on wire rack for 10 minutes; remove from casserole and cool completely on rack.

VARIATION: *Irish Soda Bread with Raisins: prepare bread as instructed above except reduce flour to 4 cups. In step 2, add 1½ cups raisins to the flour mixture before stirring in buttermilk and eggs.*

Liberty Plaza, Philadelphia

Swedish Rye Bread

2 packages active dry yeast
1½ cups warm water (105–115°F)
⅓ cup brown sugar
⅓ cup molasses
1 tablespoon salt
1 tablespoon anise seed or fennel seed, crushed
1 tablespoon shredded orange zest
2 tablespoons vegetable oil, plus more for bowl
2½ cups medium rye flour
2¼–2¾ cups all-purpose flour

MAKES 2 LOAVES

1. In a large bowl, dissolve yeast in warm water. Mix in brown sugar, molasses, salt, anise seed, orange zest, oil and rye flour. Mix until smooth. Stir in enough all-purpose flour to form a soft dough.

2. Turn dough onto a lightly floured surface. Cover with a towel and allow to rest for 10 to 15 minutes. Remove towel and knead until smooth and elastic, about 5 minutes. Place dough in a greased bowl and roll to coat. Cover with towel and let rise in a warm place until dough doubles in size, about 1 hour. Dough is ready when an indentation remains when touched.

3. Punch down dough and divide into halves. Shape each half into a round, slightly flat loaf. Place loaves on opposite corners of a greased cookie sheet. Cover and let rise until double in size, about 1 hour.

4. Heat oven to 375°F. Bake until loaves sound hollow when tapped, 40 to 50 minutes. Cool on wire rack.

French Chocolate Custard

SERVES 6

1. Preheat oven to 350°F.

2. In a medium pot over low heat, mix together half-and-half and chocolate chips, stirring constantly, until chocolate is melted and mixture is smooth. Cool slightly.

3. In a bowl, beat together eggs, ⅓ cup sugar and salt and gradually stir into cooled chocolate mixture, stirring constantly. Pour into 6 custard cups or 6 ovenproof pot de crème cups.

4. Place cups into a baking pan on oven rack. Create a water bath by pouring boiling water into the pan to within ½ inch of the top of cups. Bake for 20 to 25 minutes. Remove cups from water and cool slightly. Cover and refrigerate at least 4 hours but no longer than 24 hours.

5. In a bowl, beat together whipping cream and 1 tablespoon sugar until stiff; fold in brandy. To serve, top each custard with whipped cream.

1½ cups half-and-half
1 package (6 ounce) semisweet chocolate chips
3 eggs
⅓ cup plus 1 tablespoon sugar
⅛ teaspoon salt
½ cup whipping cream
1 tablespoon sugar
2 tablespoons brandy, orange-flavored liqueur or crème de menthe (optional)

Irish Coffee

1 short-stemmed,
tulip-shaped glass
3 cubes sugar (about 3 teaspoons)
¾ cup hot black coffee
1 jigger Irish whiskey
¼ cup heavy cream, lightly
whipped

This delicious recipe comes from San Francisco's Buena Vista Bar. When we fix it, we imagine that we're sitting and sipping in one of our favorite cities in the world!

MAKES 1 DRINK

1. Preheat the glass by filling with hot water and allowing it to stand for 1 to 2 minutes before emptying.

2. Place sugar into glass and fill immediately about three-quarters full with very hot coffee, stirring until sugar is completely dissolved. Add Irish whiskey and top with whipped cream. Serve immediately, while drink is piping hot.

Emerald Isle

Looking
for
Memories

Aebleskivers or Pancakes

BASIC AEBLSKIVER:

2   cups all-purpose flour
1   teaspoon baking powder
1   teaspoon baking soda
4   eggs, separated
1   tablespoon sugar
½   teaspoon salt
2   scant cups milk
¼   cup butter, melted
Powdered sugar

SERVES 6

1. In a bowl, combine flour, baking soda and baking powder. In a separate bowl, beat egg yolks; add sugar, salt, milk and dry ingredients and mix thoroughly.

2. Whisk together egg whites until stiff peaks form and fold into batter.

3. Heat an Aebleskiver pan (or griddle) over medium heat. Brush melted butter into each depression and fill with batter; cook until small bubbles appear. Use a spoon to turn the Aebleskiver over and cook the other side until golden brown. To serve, sprinkle with powdered sugar.

NOTE: *If desired, add a small slice of apple or a teaspoon of applesauce to the batter before it is turned. It will sink into the batter.*

Variations

Follow the directions for Basic Aebleskiver for these variations.

BUTTERMILK AEBLESKIVER:

2   cups all-purpose flour
1   teaspoon baking powder
1   teaspoon baking soda
3   eggs, separated
2   tablespoons sugar
½   teaspoon salt
2   cups buttermilk
¼   cup butter, melted
Powdered sugar

SOUR CREAM AEBLESKIVER:

2   cups all-purpose flour, sifted
1   teaspoon baking powder
1   teaspoon baking soda
3   eggs, separated
2   tablespoons sugar
½   teaspoon ground cardamom
      (or 1 teaspoon vanilla)
¼   teaspoon salt
1   cup sour cream
⅔   cup milk
¼   cup butter, melted

Almost Heaven

Oatmeal Nut Waffles

1½ cups whole wheat flour
2   teaspoons baking powder
½   tablespoon salt
2   cups milk
2   eggs
4   tablespoons butter, melted
2   tablespoons honey
1   cup rolled oats (not the instant kind)
1   cup chopped walnuts

MAKES 12 WAFFLES

1. In medium bowl, mix together flour, baking powder and salt. Mix milk, eggs, butter and honey and beat until smooth. Stir in the dry ingredients then stir in oats and nuts.

2. Cook in an ungreased waffle iron until golden brown. If desired, serve with butter and honey.

The Valley of Peace

Guardian Castle

Scones

MAKES 12

1. Preheat oven to 450°F. Grease a baking sheet with butter.

2. Combine butter with sour cream, milk and egg. Stir in flour and salt. Mix thoroughly into to a smooth dough. Turn out onto work surface, knead briefly and flatten by hand to ¾-inch thick. Cut with a 2-inch cookie cutter and place on prepared pan. Bake for 10 to12 minutes, until slightly golden brown.

4 tablespoons butter, melted and cooled, plus extra for pan

½ cup sour cream

¼ cup milk

1 egg

2 cups self-rising flour

⅛ teaspoon salt

Blueberry Orange Scones

2¾ cups all-purpose flour
⅔ cup sugar
1 tablespoon baking powder
1 teaspoon baking soda
¾ teaspoon salt
6 tablespoons cold unsalted butter, cut into small cubes
1 tablespoon white vinegar
1 cup milk
1 teaspoon freshly grated orange zest
1 egg
1 cup fresh blueberries
1 egg white
2 tablespoons granulated sugar

MAKES 12

1. Preheat oven to 400°F. Line a baking sheet with parchment paper or a silicone mat.

2. In a bowl, combine flour, sugar, baking powder, baking soda and salt. Add butter and mix with pastry blender until mixture resembles coarse crumbs. Stir in vinegar, milk, zest and egg, until just combined. Gently stir in blueberries.

3. Using a ½ cup ice-cream scoop, drop heaping scoopfuls of dough onto prepared sheet, about 2-inches apart. Brush with egg white and sprinkle with sugar.

4. Bake for 12 to 15 minutes, until golden brown. Remove to wire rack to cool slightly. Serve warm or at room temperature with flavored preserves, if desired.

Bran Flax Muffins

MAKES 12

1. Preheat oven to 350°F. Line a muffin pan with paper muffin cups.

2. In a bowl, mix together flour, flaxseed meal, oat bran, brown sugar, baking soda, baking powder, salt and cinnamon. In a separate bowl, mix together milk, eggs and vanilla. Mix with dry ingredients. Add carrots, apples, and, if using, raisins and nuts. Stir until just combined.

3. Divide batter evenly into muffin cups and bake for 15 to 20 minutes, until a toothpick inserted into the middle comes out clean.

4. Remove from the oven and cool on a rack.

1½	cups all-purpose flour
¾	cup flaxseed meal (I recommend Bob's Red Mill brand)
¾	cup oat bran
1	cup brown sugar
2	teaspoons baking soda
1	teaspoon baking powder
½	teaspoon salt
2	teaspoons ground cinnamon
¾	cup milk
2	eggs
1	teaspoon vanilla
1½	cups shredded carrots
2	apples, peeled and shredded
½	cup raisins (optional)
1	cup chopped nuts (optional)

Banana Nut Muffins for a Crowd

20 cups all-purpose flour
5 teaspoons baking soda
5 tablespoons baking powder
5 teaspoons salt
¼ cup (1 stick) softened butter
10 cups sugar
2 quarts milk
12 eggs
2 tablespoons vanilla
20 very ripe bananas, mashed

*W*here do I find so many bananas? We always freeze our overripe bananas, so we'll have them for muffins and breads later.

MAKES 8 DOZEN

1. Preheat oven to 325°F. Line muffin pans with paper muffin cups.

2. In a very large bowl, mix together flour, baking soda, baking powder and salt. In a separate bowl, cream together butter with some of the sugar. Add remaining sugar, milk, eggs, vanilla and bananas and mix thoroughly. Mix with dry ingredients.

3. Using an ice cream scooper, fill muffin cups with one scoop batter and bake for 35 minutes, in batches if necessary, until a toothpick inserted into the middle comes out clean.

4. Remove from the oven and cool on a rack.

Granola

2 cups rolled oats
¼ cup brown sugar
¼ cup vegetable oil
¼ cup water
¼ teaspoon ground cinnamon
⅓ teaspoon salt
½ cup almonds
1 teaspoon vanilla

*M*y Mom, Nancy, always makes this in a big batch. I loved it for breakfast or snacks when I was a girl; my girls love it now. This has always been one of my Dad, Ed Willey's, favorites!

1. Preheat oven to 300°F.

2. Combine the ingredients in a bowl and mix thoroughly. Spread mixture onto a baking sheet and cook, stirring often, for 30 minutes until golden brown.

Heather's Hutch

Hummus

1 can (15 ounce) garbanzos, drained with liquid reserved
¼ cup tahini (sesame paste; or ¼ cup toasted sesame seeds), plus 2 tablespoons olive oil
3 tablespoons freshly squeezed lemon juice
1 clove garlic, smashed
¼ teaspoon ground cumin
Salt
Black pepper
Optional garnishes: olive oil and chopped fresh parsley

We recently went to the Holy Land for the first time—and it was an incredible experience! The food was an unexpected treat, and our favorite was Hummus. Talk about healthy eating that's delicious too.

SERVES 8

1. Place garbanzos into a blender or food processor. Add tahini or, if using, toasted sesame seeds and olive oil, lemon juice, garlic, cumin and ¼ cup of the reserved garbanzo liquid. Puree, adding more garbanzo liquid if needed, until mixture is smooth and the consistency of a heavy batter. Season with salt and pepper. Garnish with olive oil and chopped parsley.

Blender Pesto

MAKES 1 CUP

1. Place all the ingredients except cheese into a blender. Puree until thoroughly combined. Pour into a bowl and stir in cheese.

NOTE: *Pesto can be prepared and stored in the refrigerator for up to one week. When using over pasta, thin with 1 tablespoon of the pasta cooking water.*

2 cups fresh basil leaves
½ cup olive oil
2 tablespoons pine nuts
2 cloves garlic, crushed
1 teaspoon salt
½ cup grated Parmesan cheese

Summer Baked Stuffed Zucchini

My Mom and Dad always had a huge garden every summer. We all know what happens with zucchini—there's so much of it! We were always looking for creative ways to use it—and this became a family favorite. Now I use the recipe—and Thom and the girls look forward to it. If your kids aren't fond of zucchini, try this!

SERVES 4

1. Preheat oven to 350°F.

2. Using a spoon, remove seeds and some flesh from the zucchini halves. Chop the seeds and flesh and set aside.

3. In a skillet, heat oil and cook garlic and onion until onion is translucent, about 3 minutes. Add reserved pulp, shredded zucchini, tomatoes and sun-dried tomatoes and continue cooking, stirring constantly, for 3 more minutes. Add Parmesan cheese and parsley and season with salt and pepper. Remove from heat.

4. Place zucchini halves in a baking dish and fill each cavity with one-fourth of the cooked zucchini mixture. Sprinkle with bread crumbs and bake for 15 to 20 minutes, until tops are golden brown. If desired, top with mozzarella cheese before cooking and serve with your favorite marinara sauce.

3 medium zucchini, 2 cut in half lengthwise and 1 shredded
¼ cup olive oil
1 clove garlic, minced
1 medium onion, chopped
1 medium tomato, chopped
2 sun-dried tomatoes (optional)
2 tablespoons grated Parmesan cheese
1 tablespoon chopped fresh parsley
2 tablespoons bread crumbs
Salt
Black pepper

Collector Recipe: Crab Cakes

1 pound crabmeat
1 tablespoon margarine
4 cloves garlic, chopped
½ cup chopped green onions
¼ cup chopped fresh parsley
1 tablespoon Old Bay
   Seafood Seasoning
¼ teaspoon salt
¼ teaspoon black pepper
¼ teaspoon chopped basil
¾ cup heavy cream
¾ cup seasoned bread crumbs

Remoulade Sauce (see opposite page)

This recipe is a reminder to me of better times in New Orleans before Hurricane Katrina. We have since relocated to Arkansas, but I still prepare this dish for my wife whenever she feels homesick!

SERVES 5–6

1. Pick through crab meat, removing pieces of shells. Set aside.

2. Over medium heat, melt margarine in a medium sauce pan. Sauté garlic in butter until golden brown. Add green onions and cook until soft. Add parsley and cook for 1 minute. Add crabmeat to pan and stir. Add dry ingredients and mix thoroughly. Add heavy cream and mix well. Add bread crumbs and mix well. The mixture should not be liquidly. Allow mixture to cool.

3. To make the crab cakes, form 3-inch size cakes, and place on a foil-lined baking sheet. Refrigerate for at least 2 hours, allowing the cakes to be firm.

4. Heat deep fryer to 365°F or preheat skilled on the stovetop to medium heat. For stovetop, spray both sides of cakes with olive oil cooking spray and cook for about 7 minutes, turning several times until golden brown. For deep fryer, dip cakes in a mixture of milk and egg, then coat with seasoned bread crumbs. Fry for about 3 minutes, turning over on each side until golden brown. Serve with Remoulade Sauce.

Recipe and Memory by Tommy Centola

Remoulade Sauce

1. Mix together vinegar, horseradish, cayenne, ketchup, garlic and salt. Add oil slowly, beating well. Add celery and green onions.

2. Keep refrigerated until ready to serve with crab cakes.

½ cup tarragon vinegar
4 tablespoons horseradish mustard
½ teaspoon cayenne pepper
2 tablespoons ketchup
1 clove garlic, chopped
1 teaspoon salt
1 tablespoon paprika
1 cup salad oil
½ cup chopped celery
½ cup chopped green onions

Pine Cove Cottage

The End of a Perfect Day III

Broccoli Chicken & Rice Casserole

SERVES 6

1. In a stockpot, heat oil and cook onion with sliced mushrooms until onions are translucent and mushrooms are tender. Add the rice, chicken, broccoli florets, cheese and mushroom soup and mix thoroughly.

2. Pour mixture into a casserole pan and top with more grated cheese. Microwave to heat thoroughly, about 3 minutes.

NOTE: *Portobello mushroom soup can be found in well-stocked grocery stores such as Whole Foods.*

1	tablespoon butter
½	onion, chopped
1	cup sliced mushrooms
4	cups cooked brown rice
2	cups cooked chicken
2	cups cooked broccoli florets
1	cup shredded Monterey Jack and cheddar cheese
1	carton (16 ounce) portobello mushroom soup

El Dorado Beef Casserole

½   pound ground beef
1   medium onion, chopped
¼   teaspoon chili powder
2   cans (8 ounces each) tomato sauce
½   pound Monterey Jack cheese, grated
1   container (8 ounce) sour cream
1   bag tortilla chips, crush

Thom's mother, Mary Anne, created this recipe when he was a young boy. It was his favorite, and he would always request it for his birthday. He still asks for it from time to time.

SERVES 6

1. Preheat oven to 375°F.

2. In a skillet over medium heat, brown the meat with the onion. Season with chili powder. Add tomato sauce and 1 can (8 ounce) full of water. Simmer for 2 or 3 minutes.

3. Place one-third of the meat mixture into a baking dish. Top with one-third of the crushed chips, one-third of the sour cream and one-third of the cheese. Repeat layering process two more times.

4. Bake for about 30 minutes until bubbly.

Pigs in a Blanket

These are a New Year's Eve tradition at our house. And I know that a few New Years' celebrations have gone by because my girls have taken over making this family favorite!

MAKES 4 DOZEN

1. Preheat oven to 375°F.

2. Using a knife, slit wieners to within ½ inch of ends and stuff with strips of cheese. Place frank on shortest side of dough triangle and roll up. Place, cheese-side-up, on a baking sheet. Bake for 12 to 15 minutes or until golden brown. Serve with grainy mustard, if desired.

2 cans (8 ounces each) refrigerated quick crescent dinner rolls
1 package (16 ounce) cocktail franks
4 ounces sharp cheddar cheese, sliced into strips

Clearing Storms

Mom's Sloppy Joes

SERVES 6

1. In a skillet over medium heat, add oil and cook the beef and the onion until the beef browns. Add the soup, mustard and pepper and cook for 5 minutes, stirring occasionally.

2. Split and toast your favorite buns. Spoon mixture on top and serve immediately.

Don't forget the extra napkins!

1	pound ground beef
½	cup chopped onion
1	tablespoon vegetable oil
1	can (10¾ ounce) Campbell's Tomato Soup
1	tablespoon prepared mustard
⅛	teaspoon black pepper
6	buns

Apple Crisp

TOPPING:

1	cup all-purpose flour
½	cup rolled oats (not instant)
⅓	cup sugar
⅓	cup light brown sugar
½	teaspoon ground cinnamon
¼	teaspoon salt
½	cup cold, unsalted butter, cut into ¼-inch pieces
½	cup chopped pecans or walnuts (optional)

FILLING:

9	cups peeled, cored and sliced apples (about 7–8 large apples)
3	tablespoons sugar
1	tablespoon freshly squeezed lemon juice

*M*oms and kids can agree about healthy, tasty afterschool snacks. My girls and I certainly agree about apple crisp!

SERVES 8

1. Preheat oven to 425°F. Grease a 9 x 13-inch baking dish with butter.

2. Prepare the topping: combine the flour, oats, ⅓ cup sugar, brown sugar, cinnamon, salt and butter in a large mixing bowl. Mix ingredients, leaving lumps of butter. If using, add nuts and mix until just combined; set aside.

3. Prepare the filling: place the sliced apples into the prepared pan. Add sugar and lemon juice and toss the fruit gently to coat. Spread apple slices evenly into the pan and cover with topping. Bake for 30 minutes, until golden brown and crispy.

Hometown Memories I

Days of Peace

Cornbread Country Escape

SERVES 12

1. Preheat oven to 435°F. Grease a 9 x 13-inch baking pan.

2. Sift together flour, cornmeal, baking powder, baking soda, salt and sugar and set aside.

3. Mix milk and lemon juice together and allow to sit for a few minutes to make sour milk, and then beat in eggs and oil. Mix milk into flour mixture, just until flour is moistened. Pour into prepared pan and bake for 30 to 40 minutes or until a toothpick inserted in middle comes out clean.

2½ cups all-purpose flour
1 cup cornmeal
2½ teaspoons baking powder
1 teaspoon baking soda
1 teaspoon salt
½ cup sugar
2½ cups milk
3 teaspoons lemon juice
2 eggs
½ cup vegetable oil, plus extra for pan
½ cup canned corn

Banana Bread

½ cup (2 sticks) butter, plus some for greasing the pan
1¼ cups all-purpose flour
½ teaspoon salt
1 teaspoon baking soda
1 cup sugar
3 ripe bananas, mashed
2 eggs
I cup chopped walnuts (optional)

Tastes great with a glass of milk—banana bread makes a healthy, hearty afterschool snack.

MAKES 1 LOAF

1. Preheat oven to 350°F. Grease a 9 x 5-inch loaf pan.

2. Mix together the flour, salt and baking soda. Cream together the butter and sugar. Beat in the bananas and eggs. Stir this mixture into the dry ingredients. If using, gently stir in the walnuts.

3. Pour the batter into the loaf pan and bake for 45 to 60 minutes, until nicely browned. A toothpick inserted into the center will come out fairly clean when it is done. Cool on a rack for 15 minutes before removing from the pan.

Perseverance

Pumpkin Bread

3½ cups all-purpose flour
2 teaspoons baking soda
1 teaspoon salt
1 tablespoon baking powder
1 teaspoon ground cinnamon
1 teaspoon ground nutmeg
1 tablespoon ground allspice
½ teaspoon ground cloves
⅔ cup water
3 cups sugar
1 cup vegetable oil
1⅔ cups fresh pumpkin puree
(canned, not pie filling)
4 eggs

Each season has its special treats. Pumpkin bread is a Fall highlight; I make it just as the girls head back to school. For them, it's a favorite snack or dessert!

MAKES 2 LOAVES

1. Preheat oven to 350°F. Grease and flour two 9 x 5-inch loaf pans.

2. Sift flour, baking soda, salt, baking powder, cinnamon, nutmeg, allspice and cloves. In a separate bowl, combine sugar, oil, pumpkin and eggs and beat until light and fluffy. Add water and mix thoroughly. Stir this mixture into the dry ingredients.

3. Pour the batter equally into the loaf pans and bake for 45 minutes, until nicely browned. A toothpick inserted into the center will come out clean when loaves are done. Cool on a rack for 15 minutes before removing from the pan.

Super Duper Sugar Cookies

M y Grandma Edna's recipe. She would make these for us for breakfast and serve them warm right out of the oven—and we would wake up to the smell of cookies baking! Yummy!

MAKES 24

1. Sift together flour, cream of tarter and baking soda. In a separate bowl, using an electric mixer, mix together shortening, sugars and egg. Add milk and vanilla. Add dry ingredients and mix to combine. Chill dough for 1 hour.

2. Preheat oven to 350°F.

3. Roll out dough, cut into desired shapes, place on cookie sheets and sprinkle with sugar. Bake until lightly brown. Remove cookies to a cooling rack.

2⅔ cups all-purpose flour
2   teaspoons cream of tarter
1   teaspoon baking soda
1   cup shortening or butter
½   cup sugar
½   cup brown sugar
1   egg
3   teaspoons milk
2   teaspoons vanilla

It Doesn't Get Much Better

Sun's Up Raisin Cookies

I like to think of these as a meal-in-a-cookie. When the girls are in a hurry, they like to eat these as breakfast on the run.

MAKES 12

1. Chop raisins coarsely and combine with coconut and set aside. Mix together flour, bran, baking powder, baking soda and salt.

2. Using an electric mixer, mix shortening and sugar. Beat in eggs and vanilla. Add dry ingredients and mix until just combined. Gently mix in oats and raisin mixture. Chill dough for 1 hour.

3. Preheat oven to 375°F.

4. Measure ⅓ cup dough for each cookie and place on a lightly greased cookie sheet. Flatten into 4-inch rounds. Bake for 10 to 12 minutes, until golden brown. Remove cookies to cooling rack.

1	cup raisins
1	cup shredded coconut
1½	cups whole wheat flour
1	cup whole wheat flakes bran
½	teaspoon baking powder
½	teaspoon baking soda
½	teaspoon salt
¾	cup soft shortening
¾	cup brown sugar
2	eggs
1	teaspoon vanilla
1	cup quick-cooking oats

Vanishing Oatmeal Raisin Cookies

1¾ cups all-purpose flour
1 teaspoon baking soda
½ teaspoon salt
1 cup (2 sticks) butter, softened
1 cup brown sugar
½ cup sugar
2 eggs
1 teaspoon vanilla
1 cup raisins
3 cups rolled oats (not instant)
1 cup mini M & M's

MAKES 48

1. Heat oven to 350°F.

2. Combine flour, baking soda and salt. Using an electric mixer, beat together butter and sugars until creamy. Add eggs and vanilla and beat well. Add dry ingredients and mix until just combined. Gently stir in oats, raisins and mini M & M's.

3. Drop by rounded tablespoonfuls onto a cookie sheet. Bake 10 to 12 minutes, until golden brown. Cool 1 minute on cookie sheet and then remove to wire rack.

Chandler's Lowfat M & M Cookies

These are my daughter Chandler's creation! She wanted to make a healthier version of the traditional M & M cookie. I think she improved on the flavor as well.

MAKES 24

1. Preheat oven to 375°F.

2. In a bow, combine flour, baking soda and salt. Using an electric mixer, cream butter with sugars. Add egg, egg white and vanilla and mix well. Combine with dry ingredients and mix until just combined. Gently stir in M & M's.

3. Scoop out on to a cookie sheet and bake for 8 to 10 minutes, until lightly golden brown. Cool on a wire rack.

2¼ cups all-purpose flour
1 teaspoon baking soda
½ teaspoon salt
½ stick (4 tablespoons) butter
¾ cup brown sugar
⅔ cup sugar
1 egg
1 egg white
2 teaspoons vanilla
1 cup M & M's

Sunday Outing

Strawberry Shortcake

For the Kinkade family, strawberry shortcake—light, fluffy, so good—just goes with summer. After a day of swimming and sunshine, what could be better?

SERVES 4

1. Preheat oven to 350°F.

2. In a bowl, combine flour, baking soda, salt and 2 tablespoons sugar. Add shortening and mix until mixture resembles coarse sand. Add cream and mix just until dough forms moist clumps.

3. Transfer dough to lightly floured work surface. Knead gently just until dough holds together. Pat out to a thickness of 1 inch. Slice dough into 4 wedges. Transfer to a baking sheet and brush with egg. Bake for 20 minutes, until biscuits start to brown. Cool on a wire rack.

4. Whip cream with 1 tablespoon sugar and set aside.

5. To serve, slice biscuits in half, spoon strawberries over bottom halves, top with whipped cream and then top with remaining biscuit halves.

2	cups flour
3	teaspoons baking powder
1	teaspoon salt
3	tablespoons sugar, divided
¼	cup shortening
I	cup milk
1	egg, beaten
3	cups strawberries, hulled and sliced
1	cup whipping cream

Apple Hill Cake

½ cup vegetable oil
2 cups sugar
2 eggs
2 teaspoons vanilla
4 cups peeled and diced apples
2 cups all-purpose flour
1 teaspoon salt
2 teaspoons ground cinnamon
1 teaspoon nutmeg
2 teaspoon baking soda

This cake is part of the Kinkade family's Fall ritual. When the girls were little, we used to go to Apple Hill in Northern California and pick apples, then come home and bake this cake. Of course, we'd add a few pies while we were at it!

SERVES 10

1. Preheat oven to 350°F. Grease and flour a 9 x 13-inch baking pan.

2. In a bowl, combine oil, sugar, eggs and vanilla and mix well. Add apples. In a separate bowl, mix remaining ingredients and fold into apple mixture. Pour batter into prepared pan and bake for 1 hour.

3. Serve hot, or cool on a wire rack. Top with whipped cream, if desired.

Amber Afternoon

Blossom Hill Church

Aunt Hazel's Carrot Wedding Cake

Carrot cake was the first cake I made for Thom; I stole his heart with it when we were twelve! My Aunt Hazel made this special carrot cake recipe for our wedding cake, just because it was the first cake I ever made for Thom. It's still a big treat for him when I make it now.

1. Sift all dry ingredients together and set aside. In a separate bowl, mix oil, sugar and eggs, beating after each addition. Add dry ingredients, mix well. Add carrots, pineapple and nuts. Grease and flour a 13 x 9 pan. Bake at 325°F for 40 to 45 minutes. Let cool and frost with below Cream Cheese Frosting.

2 cups flour
2 teaspoons baking powder
1½ teaspoons baking soda
1 teaspoon salt
2 teaspoons cinnamon
1½ cups cooking oil
2 cups sugar
5 eggs
2 cups grated carrots
1 can (8 ounce) crushed pineapple, well drained
¾ cup chopped nuts
2 teaspoons vanilla (use Mexican vanilla)

Cream Cheese Frosting

1. Beat all ingredients well. Spread on carrot cake.

1 package (8 ounce) cream cheese
1 stick (½ cup) margarine
1 box powdered sugar
2 teaspoons vanilla

Pineapple Whacky Cake

2 cups all-purpose flour
2 teaspoons baking soda
½ teaspoon salt
1 egg
2 tablespoons butter, melted
1½ cups sugar
2½ cups crushed pineapple, with juice
½ cup shredded coconut

*G*randma Edna contributed this yummy cake to the Kinkade family recipe book. She was a terrific cook; so many great memories start with her!

SERVES 12

1. Preheat oven to 350 F. Grease and flour a 9 x 13-inch baking pan.

2. In a bowl, combine flour, baking soda and salt and set aside. In another bowl, combine remaining ingredients and mix into dry ingredients. Pour batter into pan and bake for 45 minutes until golden brown and a toothpick inserted into the middle comes out clean.

3. Cool completely on a wire rack and then frost with Cream Cheese Icing (see recipe below).

Cream Cheese Icing

1 package (8 ounce) cream cheese, softened
½ cup (1 stick) butter, melted
1 teaspoon vanilla
3 cups powdered sugar
1 tablespoon milk

MAKES ENOUGH FROSTING FOR 1 CAKE

1. Combine all ingredients and mix until smooth.

Strawberry Pie

Every cook has personal favorites; this is one of mine. Sometimes, I'll make it just for me!

SERVES 8

1. In a pot over medium heat, combine sugar, cornstarch and water and simmer, stirring constantly, for 3 minutes, until mixture thickens. Once thickened, cook an additional 2 minutes. Remove from heat, cool slightly, add Jell-O and mix thoroughly. Stir in strawberries and salt. Pour mixture into prepared pie crust and chill in the refrigerator for 1 hour.

½ cup sugar

3 teaspoons cornstarch

1 cup water

2 tablespoons strawberry Jell-O

5 cups strawberries, hulled and chopped

⅛ teaspoon kosher salt

1 frozen prepared pie crust, thawed and baked according to package instructions

Village Inn

Rhubarb Pie

I guess I have a weakness for pies. Rhubarb pie is so rich and tangy and just delicious. Sometimes I get a taste for it–and indulge myself.

1. Mix sugar, flour and egg with rhubarb. Dot with butter. Bake at 400°F for 10 minutes; reduce to 350°F for 40 minutes. Add meringue and brown.

2   cups rhubarb
1   cup sugar
2   tablespoons flour
2   egg yolks, beaten
½   teaspoon salt
Dot butter

Blue Berry Dessert

*T*his is my mother's recipe—and was always my brother Ed's favorite. He would always ask her to make it for his birthday; in fact, it was his request on any occasion that seemed to fit!

1. Mix all ingredients in blender. Pour over graham cracker crust. Bake 15 minutes at 350°F. Chill.

1   double graham cracker crust (prepared)
8   ounces cream cheese
2   eggs
½   cup sugar
1   teaspoon vanilla

Caramel Bubble Loaf

1 cup light brown sugar
½ cup butter
1 tablespoon light corn syrup
¾ cup chopped pecans
1 package (16 ounce) hot-roll mix
¼ cup sugar
1½ teaspoons ground cinnamon

SERVES 12

1. Preheat oven to 350°F. Grease and flour Bundt pan.

2. In a saucepan over medium heat, combine ½ cup brown sugar, 2 tablespoons butter and the corn syrup and bring to a boil. Stir to dissolve sugar. Pour into prepared pan. Sprinkle with nuts.

3. Prepare roll mix according to package instructions. Divide dough into 32 equal pieces and roll into balls. Melt remaining 2 tablespoons butter. Combine remaining ½ cup brown sugar and cinnamon. Dip dough balls into butter, roll in cinnamon sugar and layer into pan. Spoon any remaining butter on top. Cover with a towel and let rise in a warm (85°F), draft-free place, for 45 minutes or until doubled in size.

4. Bake for 35 minutes, until golden brown. Invert onto wire rack and serve immediately.

Baked Caramel Corn

*H*alloween has its special treats; and, in the Kinkade house, this is one. The trick is making enough to last until the holiday!

SERVES 12

1. Preheat oven to 250°F.

2. In a pan over medium heat, melt butter. Add in brown sugar, corn syrup and salt and, stirring constantly, bring it to boil. Once the mixture boils, stop stirring and allow to cook, undisturbed, for 5 minutes. Remove from heat and stir in baking soda and vanilla.

3. In a large, shallow baking pan, gradually pour caramel over popped corn; mix well. Bake, stirring every 15 minutes, for 1 hour. Remove, cool and break into pieces.

1	cup butter
2	cups brown sugar
½	cup corn syrup
1	teaspoon salt
½	teaspoon baking soda
1	teaspoon vanilla
24	cups popped popcorn

Chocolate Fudge

18 ounces chocolate chips
(I recommend See's brand)
8 ounces miniature marshmallows
1 cup (2 sticks) butter, plus extra
for greasing pans
1 teaspoon vanilla
2 cups chopped nuts (optional)
4½ cups sugar
1 can (12 ounce) evaporated milk

This was one of my Mother's great Christmas treats! Every year, she'd make fudge using fresh walnuts from our neighbor's trees.

MAKES 2 TRAYS OF FUDGE

1. Butter 2 large shallow pans or cookie sheets.

2. In a large bowl, mix together chocolate chips, marshmallows, butter and vanilla. If using, add nuts.

3. Bring sugar and milk to rolling boil and cook, stirring constantly, for 7 to 12 minutes. Pour over mixture in bowl and mix well. Pour onto prepared pans and allow to cool completely.

Peanut Butter Balls

8 tablespoons (1 stick)
butter, softened
1 cup chunky peanut butter
2 cups powdered sugar
1 teaspoon salt
2 tablespoons vegetable
shortening
1½ cups milk
1 cup chocolate chips

Yummy! This is my sister Suzanne's recipe that she always makes for Thanksgiving.

MAKES 24

1. Using an electric mixer, cream together butter, peanut butter, sugar and salt. Roll into 1-inch balls and place on a wax or parchment paper lined cookie sheet and chill in the refrigerator for 1 hour.

2. In a double boiler over medium heat, melt shortening, milk and chocolate chips. Dip balls to coat. Place on waxed paper and refrigerate.

Main Street Celebration

Index

Credits

Acknowledgments
Special thanks to the collectors whose recipes were selected for this book:
Tommy Centola, Karen Ford Carpenter and Lezlie Cohn-Oswald.

© 2006 Silverback Books, Inc.

Recipes: Nanette Kinkade
Project Editor: Lisa M. Tooker
Food Editor: Rebecca Friend
Design: Elizabeth Watson
Production: Patty Holden
Artwork: All images ©1984–2005 Thomas Kinkade

Printed in China

ISBN 1-59637-085-8

Artwork Credit: A Holiday Gathering: back cover, 2, 8–9, 15; A View
from Cannery Row, Monterey: 94; Almost Heaven: 105; Amber
Afternoon: 4, 102–103, 139; America's Pride: 22; Antigua Sunset: 50;
Autumn Lane: 31; Biarritz: 46; Blossom Bridge: 49; Blossom Hill
Church: 140; Boston: 70; Brussels: 69; Charleston, Sunset on Rainbow
Row: 89; Chicago, Winter at the Water Tower: 45; Chinatown, San
Francisco: 66; City by the Bay: 6; Clearing Storms: 122–123; Days of
Peace: 126; Emerald Isle: 101; Golden Gate Bridge, San Francisco:
58–59; Guardian Castle: 108; Heather's Hutch: front flap, 113; Heiligen
Blut: 73; Hometown Memories I: 5, 125; Hotel Del Coronado: 7, 62;
Island Afternoon, Greece: 38; It Doesn't Get Much Better: 132; Liberty
Plaza, Philadelphia: 97; Luxemburg Gardens: 85; Main Street
Celebration: 149; Morning Dogwood: 16; Newport Harbor: 81; New
York Snow on Seventh Avenue, 1932: 41; Paris, City of Lights: front
cover, 3, 34–35, 86; Paris, Eiffel Tower: 90; Perseverance: 128–129;
Piccadilly Circus, London: 78; Pike Place Market, Seattle: 42; Pine Cove
Cottage: 117; Plaza Lights, Kansas City: 74; Portofino: 65; Puerto
Vallarta Beach: 37; Sedona Cliffs 53; Solvang: 77; Sunday Outing: 136;
Sunset over Riga: 82; The Blessings of Autumn: 28; The End of a Perfect
Day III: 118–119; The Garden Party: 27; The Old Mission, Santa
Barbara: 54; The Valley of Peace: 106–107; Venice: 1, 60–61; Venice
Canal: 57; Victorian Christmas: 10, 11; Village Inn: 144